Franka van Lent

FORTE PUBLISHERS

Contents

ISBN 90 5877 330 2

This is a publication from
Forte Publishers BV
P.O. Box 1394
3500 BJ Utrecht
The Netherlands

For more information about the creative books available from Forte Publishers:
www.hobby-party.com

Publisher: Els Neele
Editor: Irene de Vette
Photography and digital image editing: SGB | Sirius Hobby bv, Eindhoven, The Netherlands
Cover and inner design:
SGB | Sirius Hobby bv, Eindhoven, The Netherlands
Translation: TextCase Book Productions, Michael Ford

Preface

The title CreaEasy expresses the craft exactly. You can, of course, already have a lot of fun making cards using the CreaEasy templates, the CreaEasy paper and the detail sheets. The detail sheets help to give your CreaEasy pictures extra depth. Combine the detail pictures with normal pictures for a nice contrast.

The CreaEasy templates offer many more possibilities. You can decorate a wooden object or even a piece of fabric. There are two chapters devoted to this. So, as you can see, you can definitely have fun with the CreaEasy templates.

Of course, there are also six chapters in this book full of cards: pop-up cards which really make the CreaEasy cards stand out, Scrabble cards on which you can make Scrabble stones using the shape templates and to which you can add letters with a suitable picture, and Scenery cards with the pictures placed in front of and behind each other to create a scene.

Have fun with CreaEasy!

Franka

Techniques

Use plain (not high-gloss) paper without a texture to make a CreaEasy picture. The raised parts of textured paper become darker than the lower parts and this, for example, creates an unnatural flower with a chequered pattern.

Making the CreaEasy pictures

1. Place part 1 of the CreaEasy template (according to the instructions included in the packaging) on the card.
2. Rub the sponge stick over the chalk tablet.
3. Next, rub the sponge stick over the part of the template that you wish to use, from the outside to the inside. Always rub from the template towards the paper, so that the colour will change from dark to light and create a shadow effect. Rub the chalk into the paper, so that you can no longer rub it away with your finger. Blow away any loose pieces that remain on the paper. If there is a smudge, you can rub it out using an eraser.
4. Continue with step 2 of the instructions. Place part 2 in the correct position against part 1, which you have just made. Since the template is transparent, it is very easy to place the template in the correct position.
5. Again, rub from the outside to the inside. Make sure the chalk is nice and dark where two parts with the same colour meet, so that the shadow forms the dividing line between the separate pieces. If, after removing the template, you see that the chalk should be a bit darker, then you can place the template

back in the correct position (since the template is transparent) and add a little bit more chalk.
6. Carry out all the steps in the instructions. A colour picture of the template is given on the back of the packaging.
7. You can also make a mirror image of the pictures by turning the templates around.

The layer technique

1. If you wish to make a square behind a picture you have already made, then place this shape over the picture and rub some chalk around the border of the square from the outside to the inside.
2. Do not fill the entire card, but only rub around the border. By rubbing, the colour will automatically fade into the background colour of the paper.
3. As you go around the border, do not rub chalk over the picture you have already made.
4. In this way, you can also place one picture partially behind the other. Only rub chalk in the area that is not covered by the first picture.
5. If you wish to place one picture behind the other, make a copy of the picture from the packaging (the pattern with the numbers), cut it out and use it as a covering sheet. First, draw the picture that you want at the front. Place the covering sheet over this picture and draw the second picture, partially going over the covering sheet of the first picture. When you remove the covering sheet, one picture will be placed behind the other picture.

1. All CreaEasy products and Decorating Chalk boxes.

2. Draw the pictures on the detail sheet according to the CreaEasy step-by-step instructions.

3. Choose the paper you wish to use for the card and cut the picture out around the frame.

4. Stick the detail sheet on the card to give a quick and striking card with pretty details.

Materials

Various materials

Decorating chalk has been used to draw the cards in this book, but you can also use (small) inkpads in various colours. The colours will then be slightly stronger than when using chalk. Tap a sponge stick on the inkpad and brush it into the template in a rubbing motion. You can even use eye shadow, because this is a type of chalk. The result has a bit of a shine, because of the sparkle that is often used in eye shadow. If you wish to use materials other than paper, then you could also use acrylic paint. Place a small amount of paint on the sponge stick. Dab most of the paint on a piece of kitchen paper and rub the paint in the template, just as you would if you were using chalk.

Gebruikte materialen

- ❑ CreaEasy templates
  Dressed bear/rabbit (art. no. 117000/3412)
  Bear with a ball (art. no. 117000/3411)
  Pumpkin (art. no. 117000/3414)
  Leaves (art. no. 117000/3415)
  Alphabet (art. no. 117000/3420)
  Shapes I (art. no. 117000/3410)
  Tea (art. no. 117000/3413)
  Fruit (art. no. 117000/3416)
  Tulip (art. no. 117000/3402)
  Poppy (art. no. 117000/3403)
  Butterfly (art. no. 117000/3406)
- ❑ CreaEasy paper
  Fruit (art. no. 117145/2115)
  Butterfly (art. no. 117145/2108)
  Bear with a ball (art. no. 117145/2110)
  Tea (art. no. 117145/2112)
  Pumpkin (art. no. 117145/2113)
  Leaves (art. no. 117145/2114)
- ❑ CreaEasy detail sheets
  Tea (art. no. 117145/2308)
  Bear with a ball (art. no. 117145/2302)
  Butterfly (art. no. 117145/2309)
  Fruit (art. no. 117145/2305)
  Leaves (art. no. 117145/2303)
  Dressed bear (art. no. 117145/2301)
- ❑ Decorating Chalk (box with 24 colours art. no. 118055/2000, box with 9 bright colours 118022/2004, box with 9 pastel colours 118022/2003)
- ❑ Sponge sticks (art. no. 116964/0108)
- ❑ Eraser
- ❑ Card in various colours
- ❑ Knife
- ❑ Cutting mat
- ❑ Cutting ruler
- ❑ Hobby glue

Detail cards

The detail sheets consist of drawings printed in black and grey.

The CreaEasy pictures stand out more if they are drawn on the detail sheets.

1. Fruit

CreaEasy template: Fruit • CreaEasy detail sheet: Fruit • Decorating Chalk: lime green, light brown, brown, orange-yellow, burnt sienna and yellow • Dark green double card (13 x 13 cm) • Paper: ecru (12 x 12 cm) and dark green (4.5 x 4.5 and 4.6 x 4.6 cm) • Foam tape

Method

Draw apples and pears on the ecru paper. The pears are drawn in lime green with light brown over the top. The apples are drawn in orange, yellow and red. Cut a square with an apple and a pear out of the detail sheet. Use this to make the inside of an apple and a pear using yellow chalk and draw the colour of the skin around the outside. Stick the detail sheet on dark green paper and use foam tape to stick this on the card.

2. Leaves

CreaEasy template: Leaves • CreaEasy detail sheet: Leaves • CreaEasy paper: Leaves • Decorating Chalk: orange-yellow, burnt sienna, dark green and brown • Dark blue double card (10.5 x 14.8 cm) • Paper: ecru (10 x 14.3 cm) and dark blue (13 x 4.5 cm) • Foam tape

Method

Cut a rectangle out of the CreaEasy paper (12.5 x 4 cm) and tear off the left-hand side. Also tear off the left-hand side of the dark blue paper and stick the CreaEasy paper on this. Use orange-yellow chalk to draw various leaves on the left-hand side of the ecru paper. Always make sure one of the touching sections is slightly darker. Stick the ecru paper on the dark blue card. Use foam tape to stick the torn strip on the right-hand side of the ecru paper. Draw three leaves in autumn colours on the detail sheet and cut them out. Use foam tape to stick them on the CreaEasy paper.

3. Bear with a clothesline

CreaEasy template: Dressed bear • CreaEasy detail sheet: Dressed bear • Decorating Chalk: brown, lime green, orange, blue, dark green and black • Dark green double card (10.5 x 14.8 cm) • Paper: ecru (9.5 x 13.8 cm) and dark green (6.5 x 7.5 cm) • Foam tape

Method

Draw two dresses and a waistcoat in a curve at the top of the ecru paper. Draw the back of the waistcoat using the body of the bear and place a piece of paper over the bottom of it. Make the inside of the sleeves of the dress using the feet. Use a plate to draw a curved line along the clothes. Draw a knot at the ends of the line and clothes pegs on the clothes. Draw the bear and the dress on the detail sheet. Cut it out along the frame indicated and stick it on the dark green paper. Use foam tape to stick it on the card.

4. Tea

CreaEasy template: Tea • CreaEasy detail sheet: Tea • Decorating Chalk: orange-yellow, dark green, blue, light brown, brown, grey, black, yellow and burnt sienna • Dark blue double card (10.5 x 14.8 cm) • Paper: ecru (10 x 14.3 cm) and dark blue (7 x 8 cm) • Foam tape

Method

Draw various pictures from the tea template on the ecru paper. Also draw some cups, some with a saucer and some without a saucer. Use a black pencil to draw the strings of the teabags. Draw the decorative teapot on the detail sheet. Draw a drop of tea falling from the teapot. Cut the picture out 3 mm smaller at the top, bottom and right-hand side than the frame given. Tear the blue paper off. Stick the detail sheet on the torn paper and stick this on the card at an angle using foam tape.

5. Bear with a butterfly

CreaEasy templates: Bear with a ball and Butterfly • CreaEasy detail sheets: Beer with a ball and Butterfly • Decorating Chalk: orange-yellow, red, light brown, brown and black • Burgundy double card (13 x 13 cm) • Paper: ecru (12 x 12 cm) and burgundy (5.5 x 6 cm) • Foam tape

Method

Use the orange-yellow chalk to draw four different butterflies on the ecru paper. Use shadows, so that you can see the difference between the various parts of the template. Use a yellow pencil to draw the antennae. Cut the rectangle with the sitting bear out of the detail sheet. Use light brown and brown chalk to draw the bear. Stick the bear on the burgundy paper and use foam tape to stick this in the bottom left-hand corner of the card. Draw a small butterfly on the detail sheet and cut it out. Bend the wings upwards and stick it in the bear's hands.

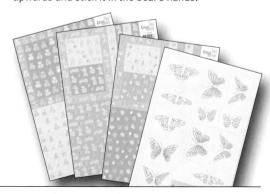

1.

2.

3.

4.

5.

Label cards

Hang one or more labels on a card for a fun result.

1. Bear

CreaEasy template: Bear with a ball • CreaEasy paper: Bear with a ball • Decorating Chalk: light brown and brown • Dark blue double card (10.5 x 14.8 cm) • Paper: light blue (5 x 9 cm), dark blue (5.5 x 9.5 cm) and white (5 x 7 cm) • Blue thread • Hole punch • Foam tape

Method

If you turn the bear doing a handstand over, then it looks as if it is climbing. Cut the bear out. Make a label from the light blue and dark blue paper. Punch a hole in the label and a hole between the arms of the bear. Weave a piece of string from the blue thread and fray the ends. Insert the string through the hole between the arms of the bear and through the hole in the label. Use foam tape to stick the bear in place. Cut the blue bear paper out of the CreaEasy paper. Cut 0.5 cm off of the sides and stick it on the double card. Punch two holes in the card and tie the label to the card.

2. Tea

CreaEasy template: Tea • Decorating Chalk: blue, light brown, red, yellow, green, grey, black and burnt sienna •
Dark blue double card (10.5 x 14.8 cm) • Paper: salmon (9.5 x 13.8 cm), dark blue (5.5 x 10.5 cm), ecru (5 x 10 cm) and white (6 x 7 cm) • Teabag label with the string • Hole punch • Foam tape

Method

Make a label from the ecru paper. Draw various small pictures from the tea template on the label. Use a pencil to draw the string of the teabag. Stick the label on the dark blue paper and cut the corners at an angle. Punch a hole in the label. Draw the teapot on white paper and cut it out. Use the circle on the tea template to draw dots on the salmon paper and stick them on the dark blue card. Punch two holes in the card. Tie the label and the teabag label to the card. Tie the teapot to the end of the string. Stick pieces of foam tape under the label and the teapot and stick them on the card.

3. Leaves

CreaEasy template: Leaves • Decorating Chalk: orange-yellow, brown, dark green and burnt sienna • Ecru double card (10.5 x 14.8 cm) • Paper: burgundy (9.5 x 13.8 cm), orange (6.5 x 10.5 cm) and ecru (6 x 10 cm) • Skeleton leaves, rope and a stick • Hole punch • Foam tape

Method

Use autumn colours to draw the leaves on the ecru paper and cut the corners at an angle. Stick this on the orange paper. Punch a hole in the label. Stick the burgundy paper on the double card and punch two holes in it. Stick the skeleton leaves and the stick just below the holes. Use the string to tie the label to the card. Use foam tape to stick the label on the card at an angle.

4. Fruit

CreaEasy templates: Fruit and Alphabet • Decorating Chalk: red, burnt sienna, dark green, blue, violet and brown • Dark green double card (10.5 x 14.8 cm) • Paper: pale yellow (10 x 14.3 cm), dark green (3x) (4.5 x 9 cm) and white (3x) (4 x 8.5 cm) • Weaving holes punch (art. no. 115635/2508) • Green ribbon (2 cm wide) • Hole punch

Method

Cut two corners of the white paper at an angle. Start by drawing the names of the fruit on the white labels. Next, fill the rest of the label with the fruit. Stick the labels on the dark green paper and cut the corners at an angle. Punch two holes in each label. Punch a line of holes in the border of the pale yellow paper. Use a piece of green ribbon to tie the labels to the yellow card by threading the ribbon through the holes. Stick the yellow card with the labels on the dark green card.

5. Pumpkins

CreaEasy templates: Pumpkin and Alphabet • Decorating Chalk: lime green, dark green, orange and brown • Paper: dark green (13 x 29.7 cm), pale yellow (12 x 12 cm and 6 x 1.5 cm), orange (3x) (4.5 x 10.5 cm), orange (6.5 x 2 cm) and white (3x) (5 x 11 cm) • Green ribbon (2 mm wide) • Hole punch • Foam tape

Method

Fold the dark green paper 13 cm from the edge. Fold the strip which sticks out forwards. Stick the pale yellow square on the front, partially under the flap, and stick the flap down. Make three labels from the white and orange paper, each one with a different type of pumpkin. Use the sponge stick to make an orange or lime green circle on the label and punch a hole in it. Punch two holes in the right-hand corner of the card and thread three ribbons through them. Tie a label to each ribbon and insert them in the flap.

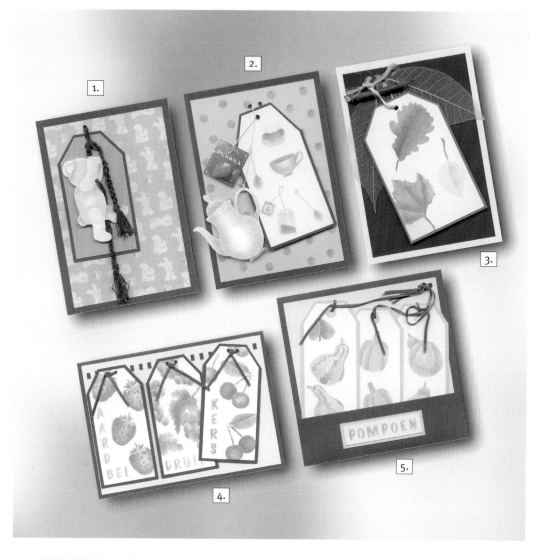

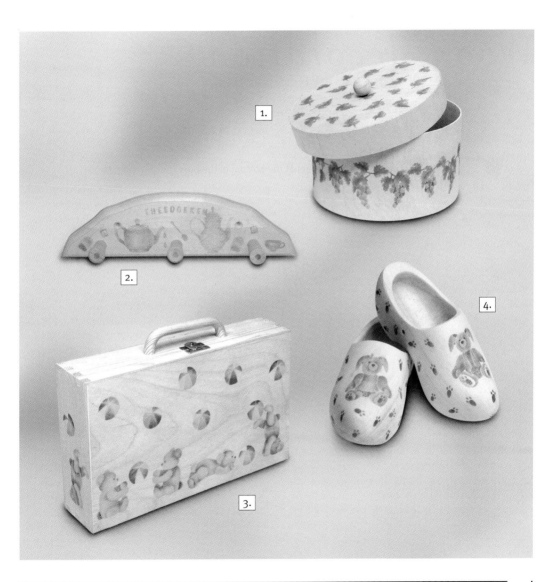

1.

2.

4.

3.

Wood decoration

You can also use the chalk on wooden objects. Once they are finished, spray them with varnish so that they do not become dirty.

1. Grape hatbox

CreaEasy template: Fruit • Decorating Chalk: blue, violet, dark green and brown • Wooden hatbox (art. no. 119125/0010) • Wooden ball (Δ 2.5 cm) • Acrylic spray varnish

Method

You can use a couple of these decorative boxes to keep your (hobby) things nice and tidy and they are also very nice to look at. Draw grapes around the edge of the box. Make the grapes and the leaves touch each other each time in a different way to create a continuous border. Make some of the bunches of grapes as a mirror image and sometimes leave out the bottom grapes to give a bit of variation. Draw two grape leaves on the lid of the box for decoration. Place the wooden ball in the middle and screw it in place from inside the box. Spray the hatbox with varnish.

2. Teacloth hooks

CreaEasy templates: Tea and Alphabet • Decorating Chalk: blue, dark green, orange, burnt sienna, light brown, brown, grey and black • Wooden teacloth hooks (art. no. 119096/0330) • Acrylic spray varnish

Method

Since the hooks have already been put together, you must be a bit handy when using the CreaEasy templates. This but it should not be too difficult, because the templates are flexible. First, draw the word teacloth above the hooks first with the word following the curve of the wood. Position the template so that a part of a teapot is between the hooks and hold it in place. First, draw the two teapots, then the teabags and the teacups in various colours. Use a black pencil to draw the string of the teabag. Use spray varnish to protect the hooks.

3. Wooden bear box

CreaEasy template: Bear with a ball • Decorating Chalk: light brown, brown, yellow, red, blue, lime green, dark green and orange • Wooden box • Handle (for drawers, purchase from a DIY shop) • Acrylic spray varnish

Method

This box is nice for keeping your cards or small things in, but it will also be appreciated if given as a present. Draw the various bears at the bottom of the box. The side with the hinges must be regarded as the bottom of the box. Use light brown chalk to colour the bears and then rub the borders with brown chalk. Pay attention to the shadow. Draw a ball between the arms of the bear throwing something; draw one on the feet of the bear doing a handstand and one in front of the bear lying down. Cover the rest of the box with balls. Do not forget the rear and the sides of the box. Drill two holes in the box on the same side as the lock. Screw the handle onto the box. Spray the box with varnish.

4. Rabbit clogs

CreaEasy templates: *Dressed bear and Dressed rabbit* •
Decorating Chalk: grey, black, brown, dark green and blue
• *Unvarnished clogs* • *Acrylic spray varnish*

Method

These clogs will make any child happy. It is also a nice idea to make a clog for every member of your family with their own name on it and then hang them by the door as a name sign. You should, of course, make a boy rabbit or bear for a boy and a girl rabbit or bear for a girl. To make the grey rabbit, cover all of the fur with grey chalk. Indicate the shadows using black chalk. The brown rabbit is drawn with brown chalk.

Rub several times over the shadow areas for this rabbit, so that they become a darker brown colour. Start with the body, so the rabbit is in the middle of the clog. Make girl rabbits in a green dress and boy rabbits in a blue waistcoat as a mirror image of each other. Cover the rest of the clogs with rabbit footprints using brown and black chalk. Spray the clogs with transparent spray varnish. Repeat a number of times so that the clogs are well protected against becoming dirty.

Making CreaEasy backgrounds

You can decorate cards with the Crea-Easy paper, but small parts of the CreaEasy templates are also suitable for making your own background paper.

1. Rabbit

CreaEasy templates: Dressed bear and Dressed rabbit • Decorating Chalk: grey and black • Light blue double card (10.5 x 14.8 cm) • Paper: light blue (6.8 x 7.4 cm) and white (6 x 6.6 cm)

Method

Draw the rabbit on the white paper. First, make all parts of the rabbit grey. Next, rub the black chalk around the border to create the shadow. Use black chalk to draw rabbit footsteps on the light blue card. Stick the card with the rabbit on the light blue card. Next, stick the rabbit card on the card with footsteps.

2. Bears

CreaEasy templates: Dressed bear and Dressed rabbit • Decorating Chalk: lime green, blue and brown • Ecru double card (10.5 x 14.8 cm) • Paper: light blue (2x) (6.5 x 7.2 cm) and white (2x) (6 x 6.8 cm)

Method

Draw the bears on white paper as a mirror image of each other. Draw a boy bear in a blue waistcoat and a girl bear in a lime green dress and a ribbon in her hair. Stick the white squares on the light blue card. Use the parts of the ribbon on the template to draw blue, lime green and brown ribbons on the ecru card. Stick the squares with the bears on the card with the ribbons.

3. Cherries and strawberries

CreaEasy template: Fruit • Decorating Chalk: red, burnt sienna, dark green and brown • Mint green double card (10.5 x 14.8 cm) • Paper: dark green (5.5 x 8.5 cm) and white (5 x 8 cm)

Method

Draw a bunch of cherries with leaves in the middle of the white paper. Cover the rest of the paper with strawberries, individual cherries and leaves that are partially falling off of the paper. Stick the white paper on the dark green paper. Cover the mint green card with cherry leaves. Stick the white paper with cherries and strawberries on the right-hand side of the card.

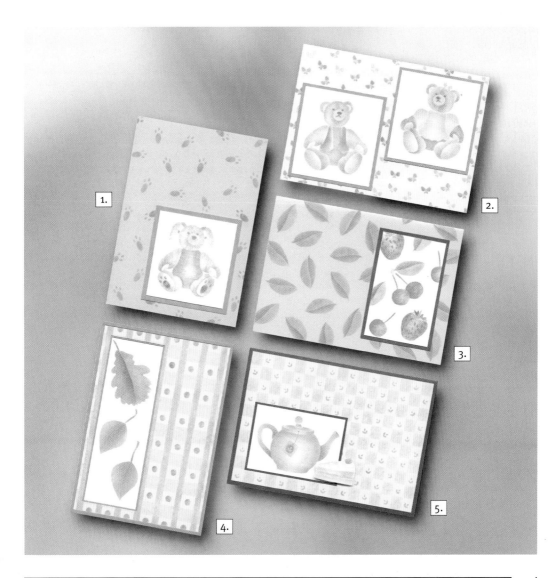

4. Leaves

CreaEasy template: Leaves • Decorating Chalk: orange-yellow, light blue, blue, lime green, green and dark green • Light blue double card (10.5 x 14.8 cm) • Paper: ecru (10.5 x 14.8 cm), light blue (4.3 x 12.7 cm) and white (4 x 12.5 cm)

Method

For this card, only the dots are drawn using the CreaEasy template. Draw short guide lines along the side of the card to help you with the strips. From the middle of the long side, draw guide lines every other centimetre, with 1 cm in between. On the short side, draw lines every other 0.5 cm with 1 cm in between. Place two CreaEasy templates or strips of thin paper on the lines. Rub orange-yellow chalk between the templates for the wide strips and rub light blue chalk between the templates for the narrow strips. Use the part of the small holly berry on the CreaEasy template to draw a dot in the squares you have just created. Stick the chequered paper on the double card. Draw the three green leaves on the white strip of paper. Stick it on the light blue paper and then on the left-hand side of the card.

5. Tea

CreaEasy template: Tea • Decorating Chalk: lime green, dark green, brown, burnt sienna and yellow • Dark green double card (10.5 x 14.8 cm) • Paper: ecru (9.9 x 14.2 cm), dark green (7.2 x 5.2 cm) and white (4.9 x 6.9 cm and 4 x 3.5 cm) • Foam tape

Method

Draw lime green squares on the ecru paper, starting in the corner. The label of the teabag is used to make the square. Make a chessboard pattern. Draw the leaves of the teabag labels going in different directions on the ecru paper. Stick the background paper that you have made on the dark green double card. Draw the teapot on the largest piece of white paper. Place the square of the teabag label on the teapot. Rub the eraser over it and then make the square lime green. Do the same with the small square of the label and the leaves. Use a pencil to draw the string of the teabag. Stick the teapot on the card, with the dark green paper behind it. Make the wedge of cake, cut it out and stick it next to the teapot using foam tape.

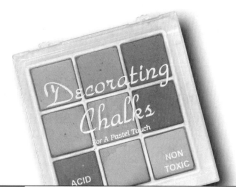

Scrabble cards

Draw 4 or 6 squares with a shadow border on the card. Draw a letter of a suitable 4-letter or a 6-letter word and a picture on each Scrabble stone.

1. Tea

CreaEasy templates: Tea, Alphabet and Shapes I • Decorating Chalk: light brown, brown, violet and blue • Purple double card (13 x 13 cm) • Paper: dark blue (12 x 12 cm) and white (11.5 x 11.5 cm)

Method
Draw three large, light brown squares on the white paper. Make a copy of the square and cut it out. Cover the light brown square with the cut out copy. Move the square template slightly with regard to the light brown square and rub brown chalk over the uncovered border of the square to create a shadow. Draw the letters T, E and A in the corners of the squares. Draw a tea template picture in each square. For the teapots that are larger than the square, place the square template over the tea template, so that you only draw the part of the teapot that fits in the square. Stick the white paper on the dark blue and then stick this on the purple double card.

2. Bear

CreaEasy templates: Bear with a ball, Alphabet and Shapes I • Decorating Chalk: light brown and brown • Light brown double card (13 x 13 cm) • Paper: dark brown (11.7 x 11.7 cm) and white (11.3 x 11.3 cm)

Method
The squares for this card are made in the same way as the squares for the tea card. Draw the letters B, E, A and R in the corners of the Scrabble stones. All the bears are larger than the squares. Therefore, first place the square template over the light brown square on the card and then draw the bear from the template. Start with the head of the bear, so that this is always in the middle of the square, and then draw the rest of the bear. The bear picture will then go up to the edge of the Scrabble stone. Stick the bear card on the dark brown paper and then stick this on the light brown card.

3. Autumn

CreaEasy templates: Pumpkin, Alphabet and Shapes I • Decorating Chalk: light brown, brown, orange, lime green and dark green • Orange double card (10.5 x 14.8 cm) • Paper: dark green (9.5 x 13.8 cm) and white (9 x 13.3 cm)

Method
Divide the card into 6 small squares using the light brown chalk. Place the square-covering sheet on the

square that you have drawn on the card. Slightly move the square template. Rub brown chalk over the square to create a shadow. Draw the letters A, U, T, U, M and N in the corners of the squares. Decorate each square with a pumpkin or a leaf. Stick the white card and the Scrabble stones on the dark green paper and then stick this on the orange double card.

4. Nature

CreaEasy templates: Leaves, Alphabet and Shapes I •
Decorating Chalk: light brown, brown, burnt sienna and
dark green • Light brown double card (10.5 x 14.8 cm) •
Paper: dark green (9.3 x 13.6 cm) and white (9 x 13.3 cm)

Method
Make six Scrabble stones as described for the Autumn card. Draw the letters N, A, T, U, R and E in the top left-hand corners of the Scrabble stones. Place the square template on the light brown Scrabble stones on the card. Draw a leaf in autumn colours in the empty part of the Scrabble stone. The picture of the leaf will then go up to the edge of the Scrabble stone. Fill all the Scrabble stones with different leaves. Stick the card with the leaves on the dark green card and then stick this on the light brown card.

5. Cherry

CreaEasy templates: Fruit, Alphabet and Shapes I •
Decorating Chalk: light brown, brown, red and dark green •
Burgundy double card (13 x 13 cm) • Paper: light brown (12
x 12 cm) and white (11.5 x 11.5 cm)

Method
Make six Scrabble stones as described for the Autumn card. Draw the letters C, H, E, R, R and Y in the Scrabble stones and then fill them with pictures of cherries. Draw the complete cherry picture in two stones. Fill the other Scrabble stones with individual cherries. Stick the light brown paper behind the cherry card and then stick this on the burgundy card.

Fabric

Use the CreaEasy templates with fabric paint to make attractive pictures on fabric. This is nice to keep for yourself or to give away as a present.

1. Napkin

CreaEasy template: Leaves • Textile Color: warm yellow (art. no. 116683/0005), brown (art. no. 116683/0017), green (art. no. 116683/0013) and dark green (art. no. 116683/0014) • Napkin (45 x 45 cm) (art. no. 002305/0150) • Ironing paper • Iron

Method

Make your own decorated napkins for an attractively laid table. Wash the napkin and iron it flat. Make a border along two joining sides of the napkin. Paint the outside edge of the small leaf using warm yellow fabric paint and the middle of the leaf using green fabric paint. Have the two colours fade into each other. Make sure the green of one side of the leaf is darker, so that there is a dividing line between the two parts. Paint the oak leaf using dark green fabric paint. Lightly brush the two parts with brown fabric paint, starting from the middle. Paint the two other leaves using the green fabric paint. Paint with the dark green fabric paint over one side to separate the parts. Once the two borders are finished, paint some more leaves on the rest of the napkin. Fix the paint by placing the ironing paper over the napkin and ironing it.

2. Bib

CreaEasy templates: Fruit and Alphabet • Textile Color: yellow (art. no. 116683/0004), warm yellow (art. no. 116683/0005), orange (art. no. 116683/0006), red (art. no. 116683/0007), dark red (art. no. 116683/0008), dark blue (art. no. 116683/0010), violet (art. no. 116683/0012), green (art. no. 116683/0013), dark green (art. no. 116683/0014) and brown (art. no. 116683/0017) • Bib (art. no. 002305/0130) • Ironing paper • Iron

Method

This bib makes an original gift if you write the name of the baby under the text. Before painting the bib, wash it and iron it flat. Start writing the text in the middle of the bib. Paint the banana using the yellow fabric paint and the warm yellow fabric paint for the fruit. Paint the skin using the warm yellow fabric paint and the orange fabric paint. Paint the pear using the green fabric paint and go lightly over it with the brown fabric paint. Paint the apple first, using yellow fabric paint and then go over it with red fabric paint. First, lightly paint the grapes using dark blue fabric paint and then go over one side with violet fabric paint. Make the grapes at the back slightly darker.

Paint the cherries and the strawberries using red fabric paint. Paint the dots on the strawberries using dark red fabric paint. Make one side of the cherry slightly darker using dark red fabric paint. Paint the leaves of the strawberry and the cherry using dark green fabric paint. Cover the bib with ironing paper and fix the paint with the iron.

3. T-shirt

CreaEasy template: Bear with a ball • Textile Color: skin colour (art. no. 116683/0016), brown (art. no. 116683/0017), warm yellow (art. no. 116683/0005), dark blue (art. no. 116683/0010) and dark red (art. no. 116683/0008) • White T-shirt • Ironing paper • Iron

Method

Wash the fabric that you wish to decorate and iron it flat. Use the fabric paint in the same way as you would chalk. Also rub the paint from the outside to the inside of the template on the fabric. You will then have more paint at the border than in the middle. Make sure you only put a little amount of paint on the sponge stick, so that it does not run under the template. It is better to go over the same bit a number of times to create a darker colour. You can also apply the paint using a hard, flat brush. Put a small amount of paint on the brush and keep it flat, so that the hairs of the brush rub over the fabric. Start by making the bears at the bottom of the T-shirt. First, make all of the template light brown using the skin coloured fabric paint. Next, use the brown paint to make the edges darker. Paint some colourful balls between the bears, so that they appear to be throwing them or so that they are on the ground. Rub the paint from the outside of the ball towards the middle, so that the edge of the ball is darker. Paint some more balls on the T-shirt. Leave the paint to dry. Place the ironing paper on the painted side of the T-shirt and fix the paint by going over it with an iron. The T-shirt can be washed at 40° C.

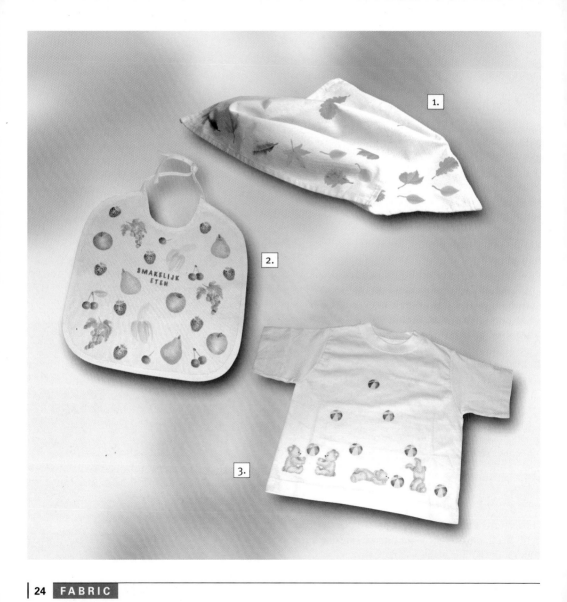

1.

2.

SMAKELIJK
ETEN

3.

Scenery cards

You can make scenery cards by placing a number of pictures behind each other. Use different parts of the same template or combine different templates. See Techniques for an explanation of how to cover the picture.

1. Fruit

CreaEasy templates: Fruit and Alphabet • CreaEasy paper: Fruit • Decorating Chalk: yellow, orange-yellow, orange, red, burnt sienna, dark green, brown, blue and violet • Dark green double card (10.5 x 14.8 cm) • Paper: dark green (11.5 x 7.8 cm) and white (11.3 x 7.6 cm) • Foam tape

Method

Cut a purple rectangle (10.5 x 10 cm) and two salmon coloured fruit strips (1.6 x 10 cm) out of the CreaEasy fruit paper. Stick the CreaEasy paper on the card. Build up the fruit at follows. Begin with the strawberry and the pear. Cover these with a covering sheet. Draw an apple that partially covers the strawberry and the pear. Cover everything. Draw the bunch of grapes and the banana. Write "Get well soon" in an arch above the fruit. Stick the fruit card on dark green paper and stick this on the card with CreaEasy paper.

2. Fruit bear

CreaEasy templates: Fruit and Bear with a ball • Decorating Chalk: brown, red, burnt sienna, dark green and black • Pale yellow double card (10.5 x 14.8 cm) • Paper: dark green (14.8 x 6 cm), burgundy (4.8 x 13.8) and white (5.5 x 13.5 cm)

Method

Draw the lying bear on the white paper. Cover the bear. Draw the strawberry in front of the nose of the bear. Draw the single cherry behind the bear on the edge of the paper. Cover everything. Draw a bunch of cherries next to the strawberry and behind the bear and the other strawberry. Cut part of the top of the white paper away so that the strip is 4.5 cm high. Cut around the protruding leaf. Stick the fruit bear on the burgundy paper, stick this on the dark green paper and finally stick this on the pale yellow card.

3. Bear with a tulip

CreaEasy templates: Bear with a ball, Tulips and Alphabet • Decorating Chalk: light brown, lime green, green, orange-yellow, red and black • Pale yellow double card (10.5 x 14.8 cm) • Paper: orange (8.5 x 12.8 cm), pale yellow (1.1 x 9 cm) and white (8.3 x 12.6 cm and 9 x 8.8 cm) • Foam tape

Method

Draw the sitting bear in the left-hand corner of the white paper. Do not draw the rear arm or the rear leg. Make a covering sheet and place it over the bear. Draw the tulip so that it is in the arms of the bear. Cover the tulip and draw the rear arm and the rear leg of the bear. Use a plate to cut the card in a curve. Stick the white card on the orange paper and also cut this in a curve. Write the text on the white strip and stick it on the yellow strip. Stick the white card with the bear on the pale yellow card. Decorate the round corner using the parts of the bear template that look like an ear. Stick the text strip on the card using foam tape.

4. Bear elf

CreaEasy templates: Dressed bear, Dressed rabbit and Butterfly • CreaEasy paper: Butterfly • Decorating Chalk: brown, orange, yellow, red and black • Pale yellow double card (10.5 x 14.8 cm) • Paper: orange (7.5 x 7.5 cm) and white (7 x 7 cm) • Foam tape

Method

Draw a bear wearing an orange dress and a ribbon in the middle of the white paper. Cover the bear with a covering sheet. Draw the wings of the butterfly behind the bear. Cut the purple butterfly paper out of the CreaEasy paper and cut 0.5 cm off of the sides. Stick the butterfly paper on the card. Stick the bear card on the orange paper and stick this at the top of the card using foam tape.

5. Poppies in a vase

CreaEasy templates: Tea and Poppies • Decorating Chalk: burnt sienna, dark green and brown • Burgundy double card (10.5 x 14.8 cm) • Paper: dark green (9.5 x 13.8 cm) and white (8.5 x 12.8 cm)

Method

The vase is made from the round part of the teapot with the foot underneath. Draw the vase at the bottom of the white paper. Make a covering sheet using a copy of the teapot and cut out the part that you have used to make the vase. Place the covering sheet on the vase that is on the card. Draw the middle poppy, making the stem touch the vase. Cover this poppy. Draw two more poppies, one on the left and one on the right, with the stems touching the vase. Remove the covering sheets. The flowers will now be standing in the vase. Draw a poppy leaf at the bottom of the foot of the vase. Stick the white paper on the dark green paper and then stick this on the burgundy card.

Pop-up cards

These cards require slightly more work than a card that is only decorated on the front, but the surprising effect is well worth it.

1. Pumpkins

CreaEasy templates: Pumpkin and Garden tools • CreaEasy paper: Pumpkin • Decorating Chalk: lime green, dark green, orange, brown, blue, grey and black • Double card: mint green (10.5 x 14.8 cm) and dark green (10 x 13.8 cm) • Paper: salmon (9 x 3.5 cm), light blue (10.3 x 14.8 cm), dark green (15.5 x 5 cm) and white

Method
Cut the lines for the pop-up strips in the mint green card according to the pattern. Make a copy of the cloud and cut it out. Place the cloud on the blue paper and rub the blue chalk around the edge. Draw a number of clouds. Cut the section where the pop-up strips go out of the bottom of the blue paper so that it is slightly larger. Stick the cloud card inside the pop-up card. Cut the grass out according to the pattern and insert it in the pop-up strips. Draw the watering can and two pumpkins. Cut them out and stick them on the remaining strips. Draw the shovel. Cut the bottom at an angle and stick it on the grass. Stick the dark green double card on the mint green card without getting any glue on the pop-up strips. Cut the 9 cm long strips out of the CreaEasy paper. Stick them on the dark green section of the card, together with the salmon paper. Draw the pumpkin on the white paper and cut it into a rectangle (3 x 4.5 cm). Cut around the piece that protrudes and stick it on the salmon paper.

2. Circus bears

CreaEasy templates: Bear with a ball and Alphabet • CreaEasy paper: Bear with a ball • Decorating Chalk: red, green, blue, orange, brown and black • Double card: light blue (13 x 13 cm) and pale yellow (12 x 12 cm) • Paper: pale yellow (9 x 3 cm and 13 x 10 cm) and white • Scrap pieces of yellow, red and blue paper

Method
Copy the card pattern onto the light blue card and cut it out. Copy the cloud onto thin paper and cut it out. Place the cloud on the section that is going to be the sky and rub blue chalk around the border. Move the cloud and repeat this. Make the circus tent from the coloured paper according to the pattern. Stick the circus tent on the two outermost protruding strips. Make the sitting bear with the ball in its hand accord-

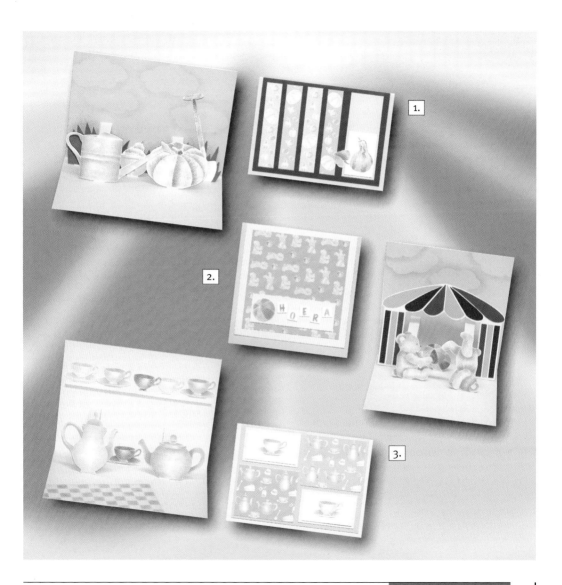

1.

2.

3.

ing to the layer technique and cut it out. Draw the bear doing a handstand and the ball and cut them out. Stick the bears and the ball on the remaining pop-up strips. Stick the pale yellow double card on the outside of the light blue card without getting any glue on the pop-up strips. Cut a square (10.5 x 10.5 cm) out of the blue CreaEasy bear paper and stick it on the pale yellow paper. Cut out 6 squares (1 x 1 cm) and draw the letters H, U, R, R, A and Y on them in different colours. Stick these and a ball on the pale yellow paper. Stick the strip at the bottom of the card.

3. Tea

CreaEasy template: Tea • CreaEasy paper: Tea • Decorating Chalk: green, blue, red and orange-yellow • Double card: pale yellow (10.5 x 14.8 cm) and salmon (10 x 13.8 cm) • Paper: pale yellow (2x 6 x 3.5 cm and 14 x 0.8 cm) and white

Method

Make the pale yellow pop-up card according to the pattern. Draw the chequered cloth at the bottom of the inner part of the pop-up card by placing two strips of paper in a corner of the card. Softly rub blue chalk along the corner of the paper. Fill the section indicated with squares cut from the tea template in a chequered pattern. Draw a blue and green teapot and a red teacup with a saucer on the white paper and cut them out. Stick them on the pop-up strips. Fold the yellow strip lengthways 3 mm from the edge and stick

it on the card to make a shelf. Draw 3 teacups with a saucer and 2 without a saucer in different colours. Cut the teacups out and stick them on the card above the shelf. Stick the salmon card on the outside of the pale yellow card without getting any glue on the pop-up strips. Cut a purple rectangle (6.5 x 5 cm) out of the CreaEasy paper and stick it on the salmon paper. Draw teacups on two white rectangles (5.5 x 3 cm). Stick them on the pale yellow paper and then on the front of the card.

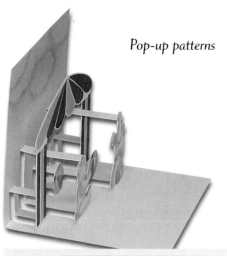

Pop-up patterns

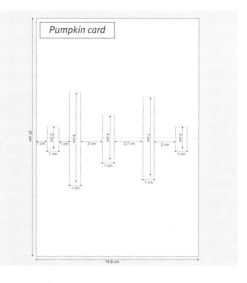

Pumpkin card

21 cm
14,8 cm

2 cm · 1 cm · 8 cm · 2 cm · 4 cm · 2,7 cm · 7 cm · 2 cm · 2 cm
1 cm · 1 cm · 1 cm · 1 cm

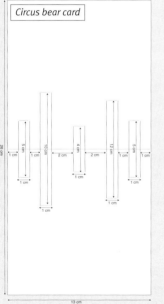

Circus bear card

26 cm
13 cm

5 cm · 10 cm · 4 cm · 12 cm · 5 cm
1 cm · 1 cm · 2 cm · 2 cm · 1 cm · 1 cm · 1 cm · 1 cm · 1 cm

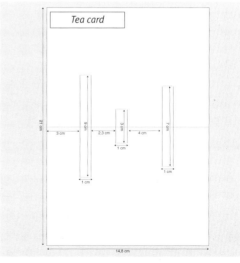

Tea card

21 cm
14,8 cm

9 cm · 3 cm · 7 cm
3 cm · 2,3 cm · 3 cm · 4 cm · 1 cm · 1 cm

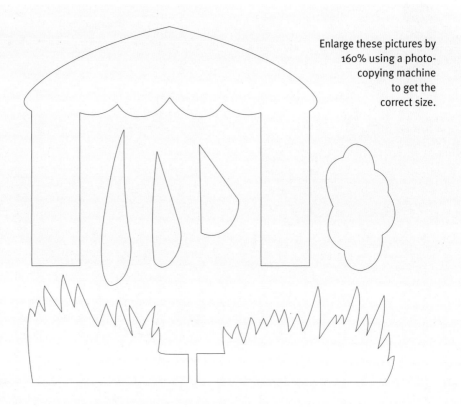

Enlarge these pictures by 160% using a photo-copying machine to get the correct size.

I wish to thank Sirius Hobby in Eindhoven, the Netherlands, for providing the CreaEasy templates, the CreaEasy paper and the CreaEasy detail sheets.

CreaEasy was developed and produced by Sirius Hobby, the Netherlands.
Shopkeepers can order the materials used from Kars & Co B.V. in Ochten, the Netherlands.